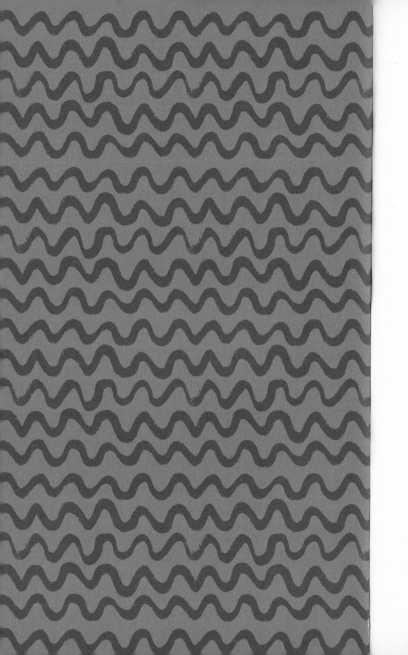

THIS IS
A BOOK FOR
PEOPLE
WHO LOVE

Hot
Sauce

THIS IS A BOOK FOR PEOPLE WHO LOVE

Hot Sauce

MATT GARCZYNSKI

ILLUSTRATIONS BY MAY VAN MILLINGEN

Running Press
PHILADELPHIA

Running Press
Hachette Book Group
1290 Avenue of the Americas, New York, NY 10104
www.runningpress.com
@Running_Press

Printed in China

First Edition: October 2019

Published by Running Press, an imprint of Perseus Books, LLC, a subsidiary
of Hachette Book Group, Inc. The Running Press name and logo is a
trademark of the Hachette Book Group.

The Hachette Speakers Bureau provides a wide range of authors for speaking
events. To find out more, go to www.hachettespeakersbureau.com or call
(866) 376-6591.

The publisher is not responsible for websites (or their content) that are not
owned by the publisher.

Text by Matt Garczynski.

Print book cover and interior design by Jenna McBride.

Library of Congress Control Number: 2019938757

ISBNs: 978-0-7624-6770-9 (hardcover), 978-0-7624-6772-3 (ebook)

RRD-S

10   9   8   7   6   5   4   3   2   1

Contents

SCOVILLE HEAT UNITS	TYPES OF PEPPERS
15,000,000	PURE CAPSAICIN
2,000,000-5,300,000	U.S. GRADE PEPPER SPRAY
1,000,000	BHUT JOLOKIA
577,000	RED SAVINA
200,000-350,000	HABANERO
100,000-250,000	CHILTEPIN
30,000-50,000	CAYENNE
15,000-30,000	ARBOL
12,000-30,000	MANZANO
8,000-23,000	SERRANO
5,000-8,000	YELLOW HOT
3,500-8,000	JALAPEÑO PEPPER
2,500-4,000	GUAJILLO
1,500-2,500	CHILACA
1,000-2,500	PASILLA
1,000-2,000	POBLANO
500-2,000	ANAHEIM
500-1,500	CHILE VERDE
500-1,000	YELLOW GENETICS
500-750	RED CHILE
0	SWEET BELLS

The
SCIENCE
of
SAUCE

T his might come as a surprise, but hot sauce isn't *actually* hot. That is to say, if you stick a thermometer inside your favorite bottle of Zombie Apocalypse (see page 105), it would indicate either room temperature or the temperature of the refrigerator shelf you just grabbed the bottle from. But pick up that thermometer and lick it clean, and you could be in for an inferno of pain. You're not delusional to *think* that hot sauce is hot—or at least no more so than every other person on earth. It's just that hot sauce *seems* hot to the human mind. And the reason that hot sauce seems hot can be chalked up to a very real phenomenon that involves the way your brain and sensory neurons conspire to perceive heat.

Capsaicin: A Pepper's Natural Defense Mechanism

To get to the bottom of the mystery of hot sauce's heat, let's first take a look at one of its most fundamental ingredients. No matter the recipe, hot sauces contain some measure of the chemical known as capsaicin. Capsaicin is found naturally occurring in chili peppers of every shape, color, or variety, all around the world. The chemical has the unique capacity of binding to a certain type of protein found in sensory neurons called the TRPV1 receptor. TRPV1 receptors are different from taste buds, in that instead of registering how a substance tastes, they detect when a substance is hot to the touch. These receptors are typically triggered by temperatures over 109 degrees Fahrenheit. Yet when brought into contact with capsaicin, the same simple chemical binding process causes them to go off in a frenzy. What the brain registers as heat from TRPV1 stimulation—say, by capsaicin—is similar to what you might experience if you plucked a hot coal from the barbecue and stuck it on your tongue.

And like wrapping your mouth around a hot coal, the sudden sensation of heat can cause the body to freak out a bit. Ingesting capsaicin brings about a whole slew of ensuing physiological reactions, which, in extreme cases, are collectively referred to as a "capsaicin overdose." Pores might begin to sweat, cheeks may flush, and nostrils might start to drip liberally. Saliva glands and tear ducts may start operating on overdrive. This is all part of a process called *thermogenesis*, whereby the body tries to purge itself of the harmful agent (when, at least in this reality, there isn't one). The body's fight-or-flight response—an evolutionary tactic for evading danger—may also kick in, causing a rush of adrenaline and an increased heart rate. What's more, the same TRPV1 proteins found in the oral cavity also occur all along the digestive tract, stimulating stomach cramps and increased production of fluids as the capsaicin-laced foods make their way through your insides (you can probably take a wild guess what this means).

In the midst of all this psychic and bodily turmoil, you may start to wonder what you could do to settle the body and mind in their moment of fiery crisis. Or perhaps you're thinking some variation of "MAKE IT STOP." Luckily, there are certain measures one *can* take to dampen the effects of capsaicin and ride it out. The most intuitive solution—sloshing water around your mouth—won't actually make much of a difference. In practice, it can just spread the reaction to different parts of the oral cavity, because capsaicin isn't soluble in water. Instead, reach for a glass of milk or yogurt. Oils and fats help break the chemical down, and the light acidity present in dairy products will also help neutralize the burn. Something citrusy, like lemon juice, isn't a bad idea either.

From an evolutionary standpoint, it's easy to see why chili peppers came to develop capsaicin. Our reaction to the chemical is all part of the plant's defensive strategy, and it's a reaction shared by other species in the Mammalian class. Curiously enough, birds are seemingly unaffected by the chemical and can be found eating freely from chili plants around the world without losing their cool. The fact is, mammals' digestive tracts will effectively destroy the seeds inside the chili pepper, while birds will spread them far and wide fully intact. It behooves the pepper to make nice with its skybound friends, allowing the species to be fruitful and multiply. Mammals, on the other hand, are cautioned to keep away.

THE FLAMING OF THE SHREW

It's been commonly accepted that humans are unique among mammals in tolerating spicy, capsaicin-rich foods. But researchers at the Kunming Institute in Yunnan, China, have recently discovered a surprising thing about the tree shrew. They determined that the tree shrew's favorite food is a capsaicinoid-rich pepper plant called the *Piper boehmeriaefolium*. In order to study this further, scientists invented a kind of special-made treat for the little guys by adding the pepper's capsaicinoids to some corn pellets. The tree shrews eagerly snacked on the pellets, while mice stayed away. What's more, the shrews showed an increased preference for the corn snacks as the scientists jacked up the capsaicinoid content.

So what's their secret? It turns out that shrews don't actually get the same enjoyment out of heat-seeking as humans do. Rather, they benefit from a decreased sensitivity to capsaicin altogether. This is due to a mutation in their TRPV1 receptors, allowing them to freely nibble on the pepper plants without feeling much of anything.

A Taste for Pain

Given all of the anguish capsaicin causes, what is it about humans that draws us to the flame? Why, despite the chili pepper's best efforts, do we keep coming back for more? What is it about us that makes us willfully subject ourselves to painful sensations?

This bizarre aspect of human nature has been explored in art and philosophy throughout history. The Buddha spoke of *samsara*, the cyclical state of pain and desire that all humans find themselves in. The desire *for* pain became the primary fascination of a German writer named Leopold von Sacher-Masoch. So notoriously depraved were his narratives of libertines getting their jollies from extreme pain that his name lent itself to a term we still use today—*masochism*. Yet the instinct to seek out pain for a quick and stimulating thrill isn't limited to nineteenth-century pornographers. It seems old Leopold touched upon a fundamental human drive shared by all "sensation seekers," as psychology has come to regard anyone with an outsize penchant for sensory input.

Skydivers, extreme athletes, and yes, chiliheads all fall into this category. And if the popularity of hot sauce proves anything, it's that there's a bit of a sensation seeker in all of us.

What happens when humans enjoy hot sauce is something called a "hedonic shift" or, as a further nod to Leopold, "benign masochism." This describes the psychological shift that takes place when a negative evaluation of a stimulus becomes a positive one. It's not that someone who enjoys spicy foods is experiencing a significantly different sensation from someone who is severely turned off by them. The person who seeks out spicy foods is simply able to understand the sensation as harmless, and even revel in it. Remember all that misery the body goes through—the sweating, crying, and drooling—in the wake of ingesting a superhot food? It turns out that adrenaline isn't the only chemical to flood the system in the midst of such a crisis. Endorphins, the neurochemicals credited with producing the fabled "runners' high," are released as a sort of natural painkiller. This can leave behind a distinctly pleasant feeling, even after the pain has subsided. Those who have just come out on the other side of an extreme capsaicin experience have described a feeling "like floating on air." That's why at any given hot sauce convention, you'll find euphoric grins on the same beet-red faces dripping with milk, snot, and sweat.

FIERY FUNNIES

Superhot foods have provided loads of inspiration for TV writers on a number of cartoon series. In Matt Stone and Trey Parker's original version of the *South Park* pilot, Cartman starts passing flames out of the seat of his pants because some older kids feed him hot tamales. And in a first-season episode of *SpongeBob SquarePants*, Sandy the Squirrel yanks on SpongeBob's tongue and threatens to dab it with a drop of "Volcano Sauce." The anthropomorphic drop dangles from the bottle and proceeds to speechify, "By the powers of naughtiness, I command this particular drop of hot sauce to be really, really hot!"

In one classic episode of *The Simpsons*, Chief Wiggum challenges Homer to try a chili pepper "grown deep in the jungle primeval by the members of a Guatemalan insane asylum." Homer downs a handful and sets off on a psychedelic (if scientifically inaccurate) vision quest. His spirit guide is a talking coyote, voiced by the one and only country legend Johnny Cash.

The Scoville Scale

The subjective nature of heat perception makes quantifying spiciness a bit tricky, though it's not for lack of trying. The pioneering method for tracking the fieriness of food is known as the Scoville scale, developed by American pharmacist Wilbur Scoville in 1912. Through a process called the Scoville organoleptic test, a spicy substance is diluted in water and given to a group of taste testers. Scoville heat units are determined based on how much the substance needs to be diluted before a majority of tasters can no longer detect the heat. The test is naturally imprecise, due to the potential variance in the test-takers' sensitivity.

In the past couple decades, however, a newer, more reliable and high-tech method has been developed that allows for the accurate measurement of a substance's capsaicin content. High-performance liquid chromatography results in a reading expressed in "pungency units," defined by the American Spice Trade Association as one part capsaicin per million. Pungency units can be converted to Scoville heat units simply by multiplying by a factor of 16.

Most sauces that advertise their heat content will use its Scoville measurement, and it's the one found in common parlance throughout the hot sauce world. (You'll find it abbreviated as SHU throughout this book.)

Yet a sauce's heat content doesn't tell the full story. Different peppers, as well as different sauce recipes, have been found to yield a wide range of heat sensations that vary in character. The heat of a habanero pepper is described as slow-burning: it comes on gradually before lingering at the back of the throat. Jalapeños will scald the tongue and lips for an instant before the feeling dissolves. Heat sensations can be sharp, dull, evenly dispersed, or localized. Fine-tune your perception of these nuances, and you'll find yourself becoming a hot sauce sommelier.

Different Kinds of Peppers

Chili peppers come in all shapes, shades, and sizes. They all belong to the genus *Capsicum* and are members of the nightshade family alongside tomatoes, eggplants, and potatoes. Of the twenty-five or so capsicum species in existence, only five are domesticated. Each of these five species can be subdivided into different varieties. *Capsicum annuum*, for instance, includes commonplace peppers such as cayenne and jalapeños. Your habaneros and Scotch bonnets hail from the species *Capsicum chinense*. There's also *Capsicum baccatum, pubescens,* and *frutescens* (don't worry, there won't be a quiz).

Each subvariety of a domesticated pepper is created through deliberate breeding and cross-pollination techniques and is thus considered a cultivar. Cultivars are most often produced to exhibit certain traits, such as sweetness or heat. Breeding the absolute spiciest cultivar has become a competitive business in the past decade or so, with Guinness regularly crowning a new "world's hottest pepper" every couple of years. At the moment, the reigning champion is a gnarled red monstrosity out of South Carolina known as the Carolina Reaper, courtesy of breeder Ed Currie. At 1.5 million SHU, it's worked its way into a number of sauces since its debut in 2012, including Smokin' Ed's Carolina Reaper and Reaper Sling Blade by CaJohns.

Capsicum baccatum

Capsicum frutescens/
Tabasco pepper

Capsicum annuum/
chile de arbol

Capsicum chinense/
bonnet pepper

Capsicum pubescens

THE SUPPOSED HEALTH BENEFITS OF CAPSAICIN

Hot sauce has long been used in the Western Hemisphere for its medicinal properties—since well before Columbus's arrival. Today, modern science backs up much of hot sauce's medicinal reputation.

 Capsaicin, the heat-making substance in chili peppers, has been shown to potentially reduce blood pressure and aid in digestive health. A 2015 study found that adults in China who regularly ate capsaicin-rich foods enjoyed lower mortality rates than those who avoided spicy offerings. It's been shown that regular consumption of capsaicin improves blood sugar and insulin reactions in those with diabetes. Capsaicin also acts as a pain reliever when directly applied in the form of a skin cream (similar to the ancient Mayan practice of rubbing chili peppers on one's gums to relieve a toothache). And some studies have even shown capsaicin to arrest the spread of cancer cells in rodents.

But that doesn't make capsaicin a cure-all. In fact, there have been cases of medical emergencies caused by ingesting *too much* capsaicin. One man experienced thunderclap headaches for days on end after eating the world's hottest chili pepper. So talk to your doctor before heading to that hot sauce convention.

HOT
SAUCE
HISTORY

With chili-based condiments at the heart of so many cuisines around the globe, it can be hard to imagine a time before hot sauce. But for the most part, the history of hot sauce as a worldwide phenomenon can be traced back only a couple centuries. Prior to the 1500s, food outside of the Western Hemisphere was mostly, well, bland.

Origins

By examining microscopic granules found in ancient food bowls across Central and South America, researchers have determined that humans were enjoying a domesticated version of the chili pepper at least 6,000 years ago. In Mexico, it was the *annuum* species that was most commonly domesticated. In the Amazon, the *chinense* and *frutescens* peppers could be found. Where exactly the idea to grind chilies into a sauce-like substance came from is uncertain. It's speculated that the earliest hot sauce in the Americas was a simple blend of peppers and water, pulverized into a sort of paste and used as a tortilla dip. It also likely served as a preservative, which Mesoamerican cooks would use to coat their meats and other perishable foods.

Eventually, the recipes for chili-based pastes evolved into moles (pronounced *mol-ehs*), from the Nahuatl word meaning "mixture." A dark, fruity variety called mole poblano is still a common fixture of Mexican cuisine, its recipe attributed to a group of sixteenth-century nuns influenced by the Aztecs. The tradition of making moles stretches back unknown centuries before then.

Yet the story of hot sauce as we know it today—a culinary phenomenon with regional variants spread around the world—begins with one of the most brutal and defining chapters of the modern era. To tell the story of hot sauce is to tell the story of Western imperialism, with special attention paid to a globetrotting megalomaniac named Chris.

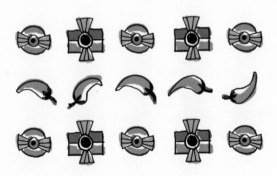

I'M DREAMING OF A WHITE-HOT CHRISTMAS

In the sixteenth century, before Europeans had ever thought of eating the dang thing, the capsicum plant was kept for ornamental purposes. The chili pepper's use as a decorative plant lasted for hundreds of years, and for some time in the early twentieth century, it was widely kept as a seasonal Christmas plant. You can still buy an ornamental pepper plant around the holidays or purchase a string of novelty chili-shaped Christmas lights online. And if you're in New Mexico around the month of December, you might see dozens of dried chili peppers arranged into Christmas wreaths.

The Columbian Exchange

Prior to the sixteenth century, most of the world didn't know spicy. Sure, there were plenty of spices going around. A vibrant spice trade sprang up across Northeast Africa, Asia, and Europe as early as 2000 BCE. But hardly anything known east of the Atlantic back then could be described as "hot" like the fruit of a capsicum plant enjoyed half a world away. Fast-forward to the fifteenth century, when the acquisition of spices reached a magnitude to rival the plot of *Dune*. In the year 1453 the Ottomans sacked the Byzantine Empire and took control

THIS IS A BOOK FOR PEOPLE WHO LOVE HOT SAUCE

of the major spice routes. The empire levied heavy taxes on product headed west, cutting off Western Europeans' sole means of getting their beloved black pepper from India. Driven by spice fever and on a serious power trip, the Spanish and Portuguese began a race to build up their maritime capabilities and discover an alternate route to South Asia.

And here's where Christopher Columbus comes in. After some fruitless appeals to the Portuguese king, he struck a deal with the Spanish crown to fund his seafaring journey to India. When the *Niña*, the *Pinta*, and the *Santa Maria* found land in October 1492, Chris really thought he'd done it. He confidently referred to the area as the "Indies," called the locals "Indians," and dubbed the strange hot fruit he encountered "pepper." (It's uncertain whether he ever learned his error before dying.) Technically, a chili pepper isn't at all related to the black pepper, yet the association remains. When Columbus's crew brought the chili back to Europe, it was grown as a curiosity in monasteries across Spain and Portugal. Portuguese traders took it from there, spreading the fruit to Portuguese colonies in Africa, like Angola, and across trading routes to places like Thailand.

In the ensuing centuries, chili peppers made their way into hundreds of regional cuisines, replacing or supplementing previously utilized spice elements like cinnamon or cardamom. They tended to become most popular in places close to the equator, in environments friendly to chili pepper cultivation—harissa, for example, became a staple condiment of North Africa. However, there were a few surprises. For instance, paprika, made of ground chili peppers, is the official spice of Hungary.

Today, evidence of this massive exchange can be seen in the hot sauce variants spread around the globe.

United States of Sauce

Hot sauce's rise to nationwide popularity in the United States was due in large part to the work of those groups who were historically most marginalized in the country. In the centuries after Columbus's arrival, enslaved Africans used hot sauce for medicinal purposes, in ways similar to those that indigenous peoples had been employing for centuries before. In the early decades of the twentieth century, the Great Migration northward of millions of African Americans helped disseminate hot sauce across the continental United States.

The earliest commercial hot sauces in the United States were introduced around the start of the nineteenth century. Manufacturers would market directly to consumers, as in a Massachusetts newspaper ad for cayenne sauce dated 1807. Over the next couple decades, hot sauce began to gradually stake a claim on the broader American consciousness. In "Swallowing an Oyster Alive," a widely circulated 1844 joke from the *St. Louis Reveille*, frontier humorist John S. Robb relates the tale of an Illinois innocent pranked into drinking an entire half-bottle of hot sauce, lest the oyster eat through his stomach. "It squirmed like a serpent when that killin' stuff touched it," cries the man. From a small handful of printed sources we can glean that hot sauce, wherever it was encountered, was making quite the impression.

The first runaway success story of American-made commercial hot sauce came in the late 1860s. That was when Edmund McIlhenny began bottling his aged Louisiana-style Tabasco sauce in cologne bottles and selling them for a dollar each to eager wholesalers (for more on Tabasco's history, see page 96). Competitors sprang up in its wake, with Louisiana-style sauces enjoying widespread popularity throughout the 1920s. Yet it would be another half-century or so before the hot sauce obsession started to really take off in the States.

Contemporary American chiliheads owe a debt of gratitude to the health food craze of the 1970s. It was then that gourmet markets began popping up across the country, which shelved exotic or hard-to-find foods from smaller manufacturers, rather than the supermarket brands. It was on these shelves that many small-name brands of hot sauces were able to find their footing in the commercial market.

Another factor in the American hot sauce boom was an influx of new immigrants from various parts of the world. In 1965, a restrictive nation-based quota system was abolished, allowing for greater immigration from places like Asia, Africa, and the Middle East. With these communities came new influnces on American cuisine, including hot sauces like sriracha and harissa. Today, America's hot sauces are a testament to the pluralistic tapestry of its people.

These days, American hot sauce is an altogether $1.5 billion industry. Small players still claim a considerable share of the market, despite attempts at domination by corporate giants like McCormick. The velocity of hot sauce's meteoric rise is kept up by a hard-core base of chiliheads who hold conventions, post on internet forums, and film reviews on YouTube. And just about everyone you'll meet is, at the very least, a casual hot sauce eater. Increasingly, to call someone a "hot sauce fanatic" is like claiming one's addicted to air. Hot sauce has become an integral part of our everyday eating habits. We live in the United States of Hot Sauce.

MYSTICAL CHILIES

Chilies play a role in numerous folk beliefs, often as a means of counteracting malignant forces. In Coahuila, Mexico, it's suggested that those who have been cursed by their enemies rub twelve ancho chilies over their body. Similarly, children believed to be cursed with the evil eye are wiped all over with an ancho to absorb the negative powers. In India, families might wrap seven green chilies and a lemon into a pendant to ward off misfortune. This pendant is kept hanging somewhere in the house for a week, before being burned up and replaced the following week. And in Italy, a *cornicello* is worn to ward off the evil eye. While the word means "little horn," the tiny red pendants resemble the chili peppers grown in the region.

Another common superstition holds that it's bad luck to hand a hot pepper directly to a friend. It could be the precursor to discord in your relationship. Rather, set it down on a table and let them pick it up on their own.

HOT SAUCES

around the

GLOBE

The Americas

As described in the previous section, the history of hot sauce in the Americas follows the condiment's assimilation by colonial powers outside the region and its eventual return to its origin. At every step of the way, recipes evolved and branched out into regional variants. Today, even the sauces that retain some native roots, such as Mexican moles, contain ingredients from Europe and Africa. What's more, many global variants of these original sauces can be found in commercialized form on North American grocery store shelves. Hot sauce in the Western Hemisphere is the product of a worldwide cultural exchange, a modern amalgam of all kinds of cuisines and traditions.

With this pluralistic exchange in mind, it can be difficult to say what makes an *American* hot sauce. Tastes do vary from state to state, but few places in the continental United States can be said to have their own distinct style of sauce. "Louisiana-style" describes thin sauces made from aged peppers mixed with vinegar, yet they're hardly limited to Louisiana. Frank's RedHot (see page 59), Texas Pete (see page 102), and Huy Fong Sriracha (see page 62) each meet the criteria for Louisiana-style sauces, though they vary a great deal in flavor and even texture. New Mexican-style sauces are made without vinegar and often have lard and flour mixed in.

In Mexico, moles are still in common use, as well as Mexican-style sauces. Recipes for these varieties may contain chipotle, or smoke-dried ripe jalapeños. The word *salsa*, meaning "sauce," applies both to the tomato-based dips commonly known to gringos as well as pourable table sauces. Farther south, in Central and South America, the ají (Scotch bonnet) pepper is commonly used in a thin, pulpy sauce also called *ají*, which contains tomatoes, cilantro, onions, and water.

NORTH AMERICA	
East Coast/Midwest/ West Coast/Canada	Various commercial sauces
South	Lousiana-style (e.g., Tabasco, Frank's RedHot)
Southwest	New Mexican-style chile sauces
Mexico	Mole sauces, tomato-based salsas, Mexican-style sauces (e.g., Valentina, Cholula)

CENTRAL & SOUTH AMERICA	
Panama	Aji chombo (Scotch bonnet) sauces
Brazil	Molho apimentado
Peru, Ecuador, Colombia, Bolivia, Chile	Aji

THE LEGEND OF AHAYUTA AND MATSILEMA

The Zuni people of the American Southwest have a story for how hot peppers came to be. One day two young gods, Matsilema and Ahayuta, got it in mind to steal the powers of thunder and lightning. So the brothers traveled to the House of the Beloved Gods and enlisted the help of Grandfather Centipede to scale the fortress walls on their behalf. Grandfather Centipede soon returned with the sacred thunder stone and lightning shaft. The boys thanked the centipede and ran back to their grandmother's house.

Once home, the brothers started playing with their new toys on the roof, lost in revelry as rain poured forth from the sky. They failed to hear their grandmother's cries for help while her house was filling with rainwater, and she eventually drowned. Overcome with regret at what they had done, they buried her, and a plant with strange red pods sprouted forth from her fiery heart. The boys vowed to spread the seeds far and wide, bringing her joy to humankind.

Asia

Soon after Columbus brought chili peppers back to Europe, Portuguese traders made quick work of spreading them around their trading routes. One of the pepper's first stops was the province of Goa, India. It was from the bustling spice markets of Goa that traders from all across the Middle East and Asia got their hands on the chili pepper and brought it back to their home markets. The fruits of this exchange can still be tasted today.

On the Indian subcontinent, chili peppers are most commonly found in curry pastes and chutneys. Chutneys have been popular beyond the boundaries India for centuries, and it's said that Columbus's ship doctor Diego Álvarez Chanca first incorporated chili peppers into a chutney for medicinal purposes. In nearby Thailand, many curry pastes can be found, which typically bear little resemblance to the Indian kinds. The world-famous sriracha also originates in Thailand and has long been a staple of Vietnamese cuisine as well. And Vietnam boasts some hot sauces of its own, in certain varieties of nuoc cham and tak kruem.

In China, the spicy peppers appear in a condiment called chili oil, a kind of chili-infused vegetable oil. Chili peppers also feature heavily in both Hunan and Sichuan cuisine, where they are key ingredients in *yuxiang* and *mala* sauces. Chilies have been used to make spicy varieties of soy sauces in both China and Japan. Korea's most popular hot sauce is *gochujang,* a fermented paste made from chili powder.

EAST ASIA	
China	Chili oil, doubanjiang, yuxiang, mala, Guilin chili sauce, duò jiāo sauce
Japan	Rāyu chili oil, spicy soy sauces, yuzukoshō
Korea	Gochujang

SOUTHEAST ASIA	
India	Curry pastes, certain chutneys
Myanmar	Balachaung
Indonesia, Malaysia, Sri Lanka	Sambal
Thailand	Nam prik, sriracha
Vietnam	Nuoc cham, Tak kruem

The Middle East & Africa

West African cuisine had already been rich in piquant spices long before Portuguese colonizers introduced the chili pepper. Popular dishes included the heavy use of a black-pepper-type berry called melegueta, as well as spices like cardamom, ginger, and nutmeg, brought in by Arabian traders. So when the chili pepper arrived, it jibed nicely with local tastes. It was referred to as "piri piri," meaning "pepper pepper," and was soon integrated into West African sauces and medicines. As West Africans were viciously enslaved en masse and brought to the Western Hemisphere, they came into further contact with the Americas' chili-heavy indigenous cuisines.

Elsewhere in sub-Saharan Africa, the arrival of the chili pepper spawned sauces like Ethiopia's *awaze*, made from a local spice blend called *berbere*. One variety called *deleh* combines oil, peppers, and honey wine. In Sierra Leone, chili peppers were included in a stew called "palaver sauce," which includes red palm oil and chopped greens such as spinach or cassava leaves.

Many contemporary South African sauces, such as *sambals*, derive from the cuisines of Southeast Asian slaves brought over by the Dutch East India Company. Peri peri sauce is also popular in South Africa, due to its significant Portuguese community.

Up in North Africa, a hot sauce called harissa took hold, with variations like *dersa* in Algeria and *felfel sudani* in Morocco. Made from bird's eye (Thai) chilies, harissa is commonly seasoned with cumin and coriander. In the Middle East, a bird's eye sauce called *shatta* developed, made by mixing ground chili peppers with oil and spices. To this day, these hot sauces define the tastes of the region.

MIDDLE EAST	
Yemen	Sahawiq (aka zhug in Israel)
The Levant (Lebanon, Syria, Iraq, Jordan, Israel, Palestine)	Shatta
Syria	Muhammara

NORTH AFRICA	
Morocco, Tunisia	Harissa (aka dersa in Algeria and felfel in Sudan)

SUB-SAHARAN AFRICA	
Ethiopia	Awaze
Sierra Leone, Ghana, Liberia, Nigeria	Palaver sauce
South Africa	Peri peri sauce, sambal, blatjang, atjar
Malawi	Nali sauce
Ghana	Shito

Caribbean

"Pepper sauce," as hot sauce is regionally known, pervades the cuisine of just about every island in the Caribbean Rim. There is evidence of a pre-Columbian hot sauce tradition belonging to the local Arawak peoples. One such sauce called *taumalin* was made from lime, chili peppers, and crabmeat. However, that tradition has been lost to time and imperial conquest. Today, Caribbean sauces typically draw upon varieties of the *chinense* species of capsicum—like the habanero, Scotch bonnet, and Trinidad scorpion—and are chock-full of herbs and spices.

Jamaican cuisine makes significant use of allspice and Scotch bonnet–based jerk sauces, often as a marinade. Much of the island's cuisine, including its pepper sauces, can be traced back to its enslaved peoples. The recipe for Busha Browne's Pukka Sauce is drawn from the archives of the historic Browne family, whose ancestor Howe Peter Browne freed Jamaica's slaves during his tenure as governor.

In Trinidad and Tobago, pepper sauces can be found made with bases of sherry or rum or blended with mustard for a sharper, multidimensional heat profile. Trinidadian cuisine has further adopted the influence of the country's East Indian population, which introduced a number of now-popular chutneys.

While commercial brands abound in the region, the most "genuine" Caribbean flavors don't come with a label. That's because the Caribbean still plays host to a rich DIY hot sauce culture, with local chefs, commercial or otherwise, concocting their own special batches from variations on island recipes. Visitors might find their new favorite sauce at an unassuming market or roadside stand, sold in a repurposed soda bottle or mayonnaise jar.

CARIBBEAN	
Barbados	Bajan (mustard-based) pepper sauce
Haiti	Sauce Ti-Malice
Puerto Rico	Pique sauce
Jamaica	Jerk sauces, bonnet sauces
Trinidad and Tobago	Chutneys

CELEBRITY CHILIHEADS

Beyoncé's single "Formation" made waves in 2016 with the lyric "I got hot sauce in my bag, swag." But the megastar isn't the only celebrity to travel with a portable bottle of hot sauce. Supermodel Naomi Campbell is reported to carry a bottle of Pickapeppa Jamaican hot sauce wherever she goes. Musician Lauryn Hill carries a special leather pouch of her five favorite sauces on tour. Supermodel and social media personality Chrissy Teigen once outed herself as a full-on hot sauce hoarder, Instagramming her kitchen drawer piled high with Cholula and sriracha packets that she keeps "for her travels." And while "Formation" was still dominating the airwaves, then-presidential candidate Hillary Clinton revealed on morning radio that she also keeps hot sauce in her bag. Her favorite kind? Marie Sharp's Habanero Pepper Sauce (see page 75).

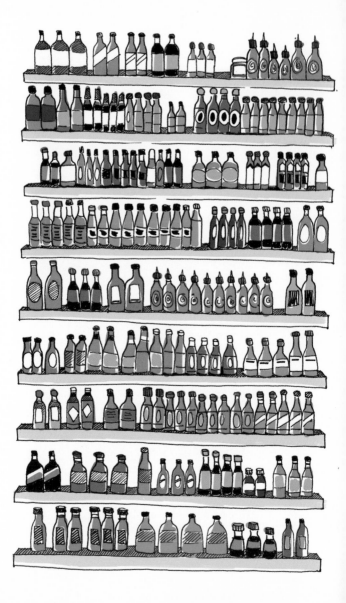

SAUCE
PROFILES

E very sauce has a story to tell. From humble chili pepper seeds to a tongue-scorching topping, a lot goes into the making of a hot sauce. Each recipe is different, and every batch its own.

What follows is a grab-bag assortment of commercial hot sauces, representing a mix of both the popular and the popularly overlooked. Many of the biggest names are included, like Tabasco and Frank's RedHot. Others are cult favorites, like Dave's Insanity and Inner Beauty, while some aren't that well-known—yet, anyway. Your all-time best-loved sauce might not be found in these pages, but keep an open mind. You might discover the favorite you never knew you had.

CHOLULA

HEAT LEVEL: 🔥🔥	PRODUCER: Jose Cuervo
PEPPERS USED: Piquin, àrbol	
CREATED: Unknown	ORIGIN: Jalisco, Mexico

Named for North America's oldest continually inhabited city, Cholula, meaning "place of retreat," is a delectable medium-spice Mexican hot sauce. It's made in the central-western Mexican state of Jalisco, a region known far and wide as the birthplace of tequila. Cholula-brand hot sauce is the main ingredient in Jalisco's *second* most famous beverage, a spicy nonalcoholic chaser called sangrita. Having become a popular offering across Mexico, Cholula expanded into the U.S. market in the 1990s by way of Austin, Texas. These days, bottles of Cholula can be found in restaurants and bars across North America. They're best recognized by their rounded beechwood tops and a folksy label that features a smiling woman in a room of sun-drenched vegetables.

The exact recipe for Cholula is over a century old and remains a closely guarded secret. What we do know is that it's made from piquin and arbol peppers, as well as salt, vinegar, xantham gum for consistency, and a special spice blend. Cholula may seem like a bare-bones table sauce, but it comes with a rich flavor that earns it a spot on countless "best of" lists. It's sold in a wide range of sizes, from single-serve packets to a 64-ounce bottle. Today Cholula comes in six different varieties, including Chipotle, Chili Lime, and Sweet Habanero. The brand enjoys a partnership with multiple major restaurant chains, meaning you'll find it on the tables at places like California Pizza Kitchen, Boston Market, and even IHOP. Who needs syrup?

CRYSTAL

HEAT LEVEL: 🔥🔥	PRODUCER: Baumer Foods
PEPPERS USED: Cayenne	
CREATED: 1923	ORIGIN: New Orleans, LA

This treasured Louisiana-style sauce shares its simple, no-frills ingredients list with its cousin Tabasco—aged peppers, vinegar, and salt. However, in Crystal's case, the peppers are the primary ingredient, meaning it's less vinegary than Tabasco—and the superior choice, according to its loyal followers.

Shipping to seventy-five countries worldwide, the company behind Crystal produces three million gallons of the sauce per year, just a hair behind Tabasco's 3.2 million. It's a local favorite in its native New Orleans, where the iconic white-and-blue label can be spotted in just about every eating establishment in town. Crystal also enjoys a regional popularity in Saudi Arabia, of all places. It was first brought to that country by Louisiana oil field workers, hungry for a taste of the bayou.

Crystal's first home was on Tchoupitoulas Street, where in 1923 Alvin and Mildred Baumer initially set up Baumer Foods. Its next headquarters on Tulane Avenue was topped with an iconic sign featuring a chef stirring up a pot of hot sauce next to the words "Crystal Preserves" in cursive lettering. In 2005, Hurricane Katrina hit the site hard, and neither the sign nor the flooded bottling plant made it through intact. Crystal has since moved to a new location upriver, to the town of Reserve, nine feet above sea level. The sign has been replicated and placed atop the luxury apartment building that now occupies its original spot.

DAVE'S INSANITY

HEAT LEVEL: 🔥🔥🔥🔥	PRODUCER: Dave's Gourmet
PEPPERS USED: Habanero, Anaheim, jalapeño, capsaicin extract	
CREATED: 1993	ORIGIN: College Park, MD

Dave's Insanity Sauce is a pioneer of the superhot genre and known for being the original "world's hottest sauce." When it debuted in 1993, Dave's was among the first condiments to incorporate capsaicin extract in its recipe. That means instead of relying on the natural limits of the capsaicin found in the peppers themselves, the sauce could pack some extra heat by drawing straight from the chemical source. The original Dave's Insanity formula clocked in at a previously unseen 180,000 SHU.

According to Dave (full name Dave Hirschkop), he whipped up the debut batch in an effort to keep unruly patrons at bay in his Maryland taqueria. In a fateful ironic twist, the sauce became a sought-after hit, and Dave began to embrace his burgeoning reputation as a culinary mad genius. He named his sauce "Insanity," even going so far as to wear a straitjacket to promotional events.

While Dave has mellowed out, his company Dave's Gourmet has kept true to its unhinged ethos. It has since introduced even hotter successors to the original formula, including Dave's Total Insanity, Dave's Ultimate Insanity, and Dave's Private Reserve—which cleverly comes in a casket-like box sealed with caution tape.

Having scorched the palates of prank victims and daredevils for a quarter century, Dave's Insanity continues its reign of fiery terror the world over. Its label still warns "one drop at a time," but for the truly insane, that's merely a suggestion.

EL YUCATECO

HEAT LEVEL: 🔥🔥	PRODUCER: El Yucateco
PEPPERS USED: Habanero	
CREATED: 1968	ORIGIN: Yucatán, Mexico

The word *Yucateco* is a regional identifier, used to refer to the people and culture of Mexico's Yucatán Peninsula. El Yucateco sauces have been made there for over fifty years, from peppers growing in the habanero and annatto fields belonging to the Gamboa family. The company's slogan is "You Get More Habanero," and they're not kidding around. Yucateco's Habenero Red variety clocks in at about 6,000 SHU—around twelve times hotter than Frank's RedHot—and its Green at around 8,500, meaning a dab is all it takes to feel the kick of these pulpy table sauces. In addition to the classic varieties, Yucateco's lineup includes five newer sauces, including an extra-hot called "Kutbil-Ik" made with a 90 percent concentration of habanero peppers. The recipe harkens back to the ancient Mayan culinary traditions of the Yucatán—*kutbil-ik* comes from the Mayan word for "crushed chili."

El Yucateco is the number-one-selling habanero sauce in the United States, yet it still may be hard to find at your local grocery chain. Seek it out at a Latin market or taqueria, or purchase a bottle online. The company recently started pilot testing its sauces in the Middle East; word is still out on whether it will catch on there.

ELIJAH'S XTREME

HEAT LEVEL: 🔥🔥🔥🔥	PRODUCER: Elijah & Bret Morey
PEPPERS USED: Ghost, Red Savina habanero	
CREATED: 2013	ORIGIN: Gastonia, NC

At six years old, Elijah Morey had a dream. He approached his dad Bret in their garden and announced his intention to be the youngest person ever to eat the hottest pepper in the world. It was this fateful declaration that sent Elijah and Bret on a capsaicin-fueled journey into the world of hot and spicy foods and eventually led them to start their own hot sauce together. The father-son duo dubbed their sauce "Elijah's Xtreme."

In just a few short years, beginning in 2013, Elijah's Xtreme has ballooned in popularity. It's won close to four dozen awards, including eight Scovies—which are kind of like hot sauce Oscars—in one year. *New York Magazine* named Elijah's Ghost Pepper sauce one of the best sauces to order online, and for good reason. It's a creamy, palatable superhot with a rich blend of roasted garlic, tomatoes, carrots, lime, and passion fruit juice. Whereas other superhots will sacrifice flavor for heat, Elijah's Xtreme packs both in good measure.

Not long after his hot sauce hit the scene, Elijah got to meet renowned chili pepper breeder "Smokin' Ed" Currie and taste the record-setting Carolina Reaper. Ten years on, he had finally achieved his dream of eating the world's hottest pepper. However, he's hardly the youngest person to have done so—successful attempts by ten-, eleven-, and twelve-year-olds have been documented on YouTube. But even if he doesn't have his name on the *Guinness World Records* list, Elijah has arguably gained something more valuable: years of quality time with his dad.

FRANK'S REDHOT

HEAT LEVEL: 🔥	PRODUCER: McCormick
PEPPERS USED: Cayenne	
CREATED: 1920	ORIGIN: Cincinnati, OH

If you were to draw up a mental picture of the eponymous "Frank" from Frank's RedHot, what kind of person would you imagine? Perhaps he runs a sports bar in a seaside tourist town. Perhaps he is the type of guy who is greeted with cries of "It's Frank!" whenever he walks in the room. In any event, you'd likely peg him as the personification of the brand's party-down attitude and general all-Americanness. But you'd be wrong because the "Frank" in this brand is a last name, belonging to a humble turn-of-the-twentieth-century émigré named Jacob Frank.

In 1896, Jacob put his traveling salesman days behind him and founded the Frank Tea and Spice Company in Cincinnati, Ohio, with his brother Emil. In 1918, the brothers partnered with the Estilette Pepper Farm in New Iberia, Louisiana, to develop an aged and vinegar-based Louisiana-style hot sauce. Over forty years later, a local restaurateur named Teressa Bellissimo spread it on unwanted chicken wings at the Anchor Bar Restaurant in Buffalo, New York, creating the first-ever plate of buffalo wings. At the time, her husband—whose actual name was Frank—received much of the credit, though history has since set the record straight.

With a relatively low heat profile, Frank's is considered a no-frills, all-purpose flavor enhancer. RedHot fans often follow the example of the brand's foulmouthed spokesperson from the commercials, who boasts, "I put that shit on everything!" The company sells over twenty-five million bottles of the original flavor every year—forty million if you count sales of all the different varieties. That must be why, in 2017, the company was purchased by spice-making conglomerate McCormick in a deal worth $4.2 billion. You could buy a lot of fifty-cent wings with that.

HUY FONG SRIRACHA

HEAT LEVEL: 🔥🔥	PRODUCER: Huy Fong Foods
PEPPERS USED: Red jalapeño	
CREATED: 1980	ORIGIN: Irwindale, CA

The story behind this trendsetting sauce is one of endurance. In the aftermath of the Vietnam War, an ethnic Chinese refugee named David Tran found asylum on U.S. shores. When it came time to name his hot sauce enterprise in 1980, he chose the name *Huy Fong*, after the Taiwanese ship that had brought him and three thousand others out of Vietnam. Tran had begun his quest to make a successful hot sauce five years earlier, with peppers grown on his brother's farm, before ethnic tensions in his homeland caused him to seek a new life abroad. When Tran was told his recipe was too spicy to appeal to American tastes, he ignored that advice, and the sauce went on to gain a cult following. That attention has since exploded into a popular movement, as sriracha fever has seized hearts and minds across North America.

The Huy Fong factory is situated in Irwindale, California, where two hundred workers churn out bottles of its signature sauce in quantities of twenty million per year. They use a jalapeño hybrid that is only in season four months out of the year, meaning bottles made toward the beginning of the season show a subdued brownish-red color, while those produced in later months get a boost of vibrant red from the ripe peppers. The facility also produces a pungent smell, reported to cause headaches and watery eyes in passersby. Despite back-and-forth lawsuits with the city of Irwindale, and after installing a new ventilation system, the factory continues production apace. The company has never bothered to advertise, since boosting demand would only surpass its production capacity. These days, the garlicky, tangy-sweet sauce quite literally sells itself.

INNER BEAUTY SAUCE

HEAT LEVEL: 🔥🔥🔥🔥	**PRODUCER:** East Coast Grill / Todd's Original
PEPPERS USED: Scotch bonnet	
CREATED: 1980s / 2016	**ORIGIN:** Cambridge, MA / Bangor, ME

After tasting his new favorite Caribbean-style mustard sauce on a trip to Barbados, star chef Chris Schlesinger had the innovative idea to, well, rip it off. He released his own version under the name "Inner Beauty," and it became a hot item at his Boston-based East Coast Grill. Made with mustard, Scotch bonnet peppers, white wine, and fruit juices, it was a bright yellow concoction easily mistaken for plain table mustard. The sauce featured heavily in Schlesinger's famous "Pasta from Hell," the main attraction at the restaurant's "Hell Night" events. Writing on the East Coast Grill website, Schlesinger credited the idea for Hell Night to "a small, sick sect of the dining public whose taunts of 'that really wasn't *that* hot' finally got the better of me and my formal training."

Bottles of Inner Beauty enjoyed indie-level fame throughout the 1990s, and for many Gen X hot sauce lovers, the name still evokes warm feelings of nostalgia. East Coast Grill shut down for good in 2017, and by that time the bottled version had long since disappeared from market shelves. Chris has broken his silence on the secret recipe in a reader Q&A in the *New York Times*, and it's available online for anyone who wants to make a copycat version at home. But if you'd prefer to buy a bottle, you're in luck. Inner Beauty superfan Todd Simcox of Original Salsa in Bangor, Maine, has recently revived the flavor in commercial form, complete with an updated take on the original label.

KARMA SAUCE

HEAT LEVEL: ♨♨ – ♨♨♨♨		PRODUCER: Karma Sauce Company
PEPPERS USED: Habanero, jalapeño, Bhut jolokia, scorpion, fattali		
CREATED: 2010	ORIGIN: Pittsford, NY	

Karma is a term referring to the cause-and-effect law of the universe. Do a good deed, get rewarded. Dab too much Extreme Karma sauce on your wings, and the universe bites back. Like many great independent hot sauce brands, Karma Sauce was named for a dog. Karma belonged to the friend of a guy named Gene, who started the enterprise in addition to his day job as an optical engineer. When he's not patenting technology for space telescopes, Gene's whipping up bottles of his famous sauce using chili peppers grown locally in New York's Finger Lakes region. Karma Sauce's recipes will also include butternut squash, red pepper, and sweet potato as key components. The line up started with two offerings: Good Karma, its mild sauce, and Bad Karma, its spicy kind. The product line has since been broadened to include multiple spicy flavors, including the now-popular Extreme Karma.

Extreme Karma is a 56,000-SHU variation on the Bad Karma recipe, relying on three of the meanest peppers on earth—Bhut Jolokia, Trinidad Scorpion, and Moruga. Its label cleverly boasts that the burn will last lifetimes. The flavor gained some online attention after being featured on "Hot Ones," a popular YouTube series of celebrities being interviewed while they eat progressively hotter hot wings (Karma once made Oscar nominee Taraji P. Henson tap out). If the flavor's following grows, Gene could expect to quit his day job. It all depends on the laws of karma.

A SAUCEMAKING REVOLUTION

Most hot sauce stories are told as triumphs of individual achievement. A lone visionary tinkers in the kitchen until stumbling on the secret recipe to entrepreneurial success. Pretty soon this DIYer is  overseeing a factory floor and outsourcing to partner farms. But it's rare that a company is willing to share democratically among its workforce. However, that's just what one worker-run company is doing in Greenfield, Massachusetts. Based in an energy-efficient solar-powered pickling facility, Real Pickles is a socially minded cooperative producing naturally fermented products out of local ingredients. Their medium-hot Tomatillo and Red Pepper sauces both enjoy gut-healthy probiotic properties, fitting with the company's stated commitment to "promoting human and ecological health." Real Pickles' goal in rebuilding a regional, organic food system means they only ship locally within the Northeast, but hopefully their success is a sign of a global movement to come.

LOUISIANA

HEAT LEVEL: 🔥	PRODUCER: Southeastern Mills, Inc.
PEPPERS USED: Cayenne	
CREATED: 1928	ORIGIN: New Iberia, LA

The simple yellow-and-red label, seen on grocery shelves and restaurant tables across the titular state, boasts that the Louisiana brand is the "original" Louisiana hot sauce. The company will go to such lengths toward convincing you that's true it's even named itself "The Original Louisiana Hot Sauce Co." While technically Tabasco has it beat by about a half-century, it *is* true that Louisiana-brand Louisiana-style hot sauce has been a cherished staple of the state's cuisine since it was introduced in 1928. The sauce is still made in the town of New Iberia, Louisiana, making it a neighbor of its elder competitor Tabasco. It is a textbook Louisiana-style sauce, produced by cooking peppers (in this case, "Louisiana long" cayenne peppers) before grinding them into a mash. The mash is then mixed with vinegar and salt and allowed to ferment for at least one year. Like most manufacturers, Louisiana uses barrel-size plastic drums for its aging process, in place of the more traditional wooden barrels. The resulting sauce comes out thin, and the heat of the long cayenne peppers—which are typically ten times hotter than jalapeños—is toned down by the vinegar base.

LUCKY DOG

HEAT LEVEL: 🔥🔥	PRODUCER: Lucky Dog
PEPPERS USED: Habanero, jalapeño, Thai, serrano	
CREATED: 2012	ORIGIN: Hayward, CA

Stressed out by his day job, Lucky Dog founder Scott Zalkind stumbled onto a special kind of therapy making hot sauce. He started by testing recipes at his backyard grill and, after seven years of tinkering, turned his hobby into a small business. The name is a tribute to his black Labrador Lucky, whose face graces the intricate tattoo-style artwork of every label. In a sign of his devotion, Scott even has *actual* tattoos of the label inked on his forearms. Scott's company still operates out of a single delivery truck, which he'll drive to festivals and farmers markets across his home state of California and beyond. The sauces have raked in dozens of awards since Lucky Dog's debut in 2012, an impressive feat for such a small operation. Scott adds each medal to a growing shrine, which he admits "is getting a little obnoxious at this point."

Lucky Dog's latest award winner is the Year of the Dog, a Thai chili pineapple sauce Scott devised after playing around with mustard sauces. Touted for its versatility, it balances the sweet and savory flavors of toasted onion, Aleppo peppers, honey, lime, Chinese mustard, and ginger. It took home a Grand Prize in the Tasting Division at the Scovies, which is like a hot sauce Best in Show.

MARIE SHARP'S

HEAT LEVEL: ♨ ♨ ♨	PRODUCER: Marie Sharp's Fine Foods, Ltd.
PEPPERS USED: Habanero	
CREATED: 1981	ORIGIN: Belize

Belize is a small Central American country to the southeast of Mexico on the Caribbean Sea. It's there in the foothills of the Maya Mountains that a team of two dozen workers diligently bottle, label, and ship Marie Sharp's Hot Sauce around the globe. The company is headed by its namesake Marie Sharp, who started making habanero-based sauces on her 400-acre family farm in 1980. At the suggestion of a friend, Sharp began selling the sauces commercially under the name Melinda's. That all ended when her U.S. distributor trademarked the name and effectively cut Sharp out of the business. She soon rebranded and started over under her own name.

Today, Marie Sharp's is one of the most popular condiments in Belize, and its thirteen flavors constitute a near-monopoly on the country's hot sauce market. The brand first began getting traction in the United States through word of mouth, till it caught the attention of the retail mega-giant Walmart. It soon started appearing on Walmart shelves across the country. The Hot Sauce Hall of Fame formally recognized Sharp's contributions to the sauce world in 2016 when it honored the famed "Queen of Habanero Sauce" in a ceremony in New York City.

NANDO'S PERI-PERI SAUCE

HEAT LEVEL: 🔥🔥🔥	PRODUCER: Nando's
PEPPERS USED: Thai	
CREATED: 1987	ORIGIN: Johannesburg, South Africa

If ever one of your "top lads" has suggested you "step up the banter" with a "Cheeky Nando's" at the end of a late night, then you've likely enjoyed this citrusy concoction before. But for those of us who have never experienced the trappings of British lad culture firsthand, this widely relished condiment across the pond is an exotic item known mainly by cultural osmosis.

The term *peri peri* from the Swahili quite literally translates to "pepper pepper." It's that cheekily named cultivar of the species *Capsicum frutescens* that's at the heart of peri peri sauce, a sharp and flavorful blend that is used primarily on chicken dishes. As the peri peri chili was spread by Portuguese traders, it took on many names, including the bird's eye chili and the Thai chili (as it's called at other points in this book).

The most famous of all peri peri sauces is Nando's, named for the South African Portuguese-style casual dining chain that bottles it. While Nando's locations are only found in the vicinity of two cities in the United States (Chicago and Washington, DC), the chain has achieved a kind of cultural dominance in Great Britain. The slang term "Cheeky Nando's" is defined as a spontaneous group outing at one of the chain's locations. The phrase itself has become a sort of meme, used by Brits to deliberately baffle Americans or by Americans to deliberately ridicule Brits.

Nando's sauce comes in five different varieties— Lemon & Herb, Garlic, Medium, Hot, and Extra Extra Hot (which will still be tolerably mild for most chiliheads). With a full 4 percent concentration of lemon in every bottle, the citrusy flavor is about as stimulating as "Cheeky Nando's" is to say out loud. So go ahead. You deserve it.

PAIN IS GOOD SAUCE

Batch #37 Garlic Hot Sauce

100% Natural
NET WT. 6.75OZ (191g)

HEAT LEVEL: 🔥🔥🔥	PRODUCER: Spicin Foods
PEPPERS USED: Scotch bonnet, habanero	
CREATED: 1999	ORIGIN: Kansas City, KS

Every Pain Is Good label features the eye-catching image of a screaming face, which should tell you something about this line of proudly hot sauces. The hottest, made with the record-setting Carolina Reaper, comes in at about 44,000 SHU. Each bottle makes the *Twilight Zone*-esque promise to "open a doorway to a new dimension of sensual euphoria."

Pain Is Good has built up an impressive catalog over the years, but its three original flavors still shine above the rest. The garlic-style Batch 37 (the one with the goateed guy on it) is rumored to have been devised on a camping trip in the Mojave Desert by the brand's mysterious "Mo," of whom not much is known. It's a decently hot 8,560 SHU, which will leave your tongue tingling while still allowing room for the garlicky, citrusy flavors to come to the fore. Batch 114, a Jamaican-style sauce, scores an even-higher 10,950 on the Scoville scale. It's made with a combination of Scotch bonnets and habaneros and infused with jerk spices and pineapple juice. Batch 218 is a Louisiana-style sauce, made with malt vinegar and a touch of Worcestershire. The unexplainable batch numbers only add to the Pain Is Good mystique.

ROSE CITY PEPPERHEADS

HEAT LEVEL: 🔥 – 🔥🔥🔥🔥	**PRODUCER:** Rose City Pepperheads
PEPPERS USED: Habanero, jalapeño, Thai, Scotch bonnet, ghost, scorpion	
CREATED: 1998	**ORIGIN:** Portland, OR

Pepper jelly is unlike most sauces—if you can even call it a sauce. It's made by mashing and boiling chili peppers and adding natural pectin to turn the mixture into a gelatinous treat. Slather pepper jelly on a breakfast sandwich, or spread it on an order of baby back ribs. You could even use the jelly as a dipping sauce for crackers and fries. The thick, spreadable consistency means it's easy to get even coverage of the hot stuff on whatever you're eating.

Susan McCormick of Rose City Pepperheads has perfected the art of pepper jellies. The Portland, Oregon-based jelly artisan has developed over two dozen flavors of fruity, delicious hot jellies. She partners with local berry and produce farmers, and even farms organic hot peppers of her own. The jellies are canned in stout glass jars with gold-colored lids, with a classic label that makes the container a tasteful addition to any gift basket. Susan's most popular flavor is her Mango Madness, a sweet and mild concoction with just a touch of peppery heat. On the hotter end of the spectrum is her Peaches & Scream, which combines peaches with habanero peppers. If you're ever in Portland, you can even visit What's the Scoop? ice cream shop and try their Peaches & Scream flavor.

Susan's personal favorite is her extra-hot Sneaky Ghost, blending ghost peppers with habanero, Thai chili, and red jalapeño peppers. Be careful not to shelve it too close to a jar of Smucker's. It could spell doom for your child's PB & J one morning when you're late for work.

SAM & OLIVER

HEAT LEVEL: ♦♦♦♦	PRODUCER: Jeff Magginniss
PEPPERS USED: Carolina Reaper	
CREATED: 2014	ORIGIN: Guilford, CT

Sam & Oliver offers an innovative lineup of boundary-pushing flavors developed by its "chief spice officer" Jeff Maginniss. The name is derived from Jeff's beloved pugs, who have inspired the saucemaker along the way. According to Jeff, the dogs' personalities inform the brand's ethos of being both nature-loving (like Oliver) and adventurous (à la Sam). Nowhere is this more apparent than in Sam & Oliver's line of natural fruit-based Reaper sauces. All six flavors combine the heat of the world's strongest pepper, the Carolina Reaper, with smooth fruit flavors like black cherry and strawberry. Founded in 2014, this sauce has been elevated in the industry by a string of awards.

The sauces themselves look like fine jams, straight from your local farmers market. Bits of fruit pulp and mashed pepper can be seen floating in each colorful dab. Grapeyard Grape Reaper uses real Concord grapes, agave nectar, and a hint of lemon for a taste like Welch's iconic grape jelly, only way spicier. The Cranksgiving cranberry sauce is the perfect alternative to that dreaded can-shaped glob for adding some interest to your turkey dinner and providing a conversation piece that's *not* about politics.

Screamsicle Orange Reaper is a complex flavor that finds an orange preserve combined with wine vinegar, almond extract, and vanilla. The flavors pair with sweet and savory dishes alike and work great as dessert sauces. So if you're still jonesing for your capsaicin fix after a main course, break out the ice cream and go wild.

SCOTTY O'HOTTY

HEAT LEVEL: 🔥🔥🔥	**PRODUCER:** Owens Family Foods
PEPPERS USED: Habanero, ghost, jalapeño	
CREATED: 2011	**ORIGIN:** Detroit, MI

Historically, the American Midwest hasn't been a hotbed of spicy foods. But these days, one Detroit couple's hot sauce could be turning that around. Scott Owens's love for spicy foods started at a young age, when his parents tried to get him to kick his thumb-sucking habit. Their idea of dabbing hot sauce on his thumb didn't go as planned, and soon enough the Owenses had a chilihead on their hands. After the financial crisis of 2008, Scott was out of work. He and his wife Suzi decided to take a chance on producing their own brand of commercial hot sauce, eventually finding space in a shared-use community kitchen to prep and bottle their recipes. Scotty O'Hotty Hot Sauce has since become an award-winning cult favorite in the Motor City and beyond.

What sets Scotty O'Hotty sauces apart most is the Beer-Bacon Chipotle Sauce, one of the only commercial beer sauces in the United States. It's a relatively mild table sauce combining what the couple calls the "major food groups"—real beer, real chili peppers, and real bacon. There's also a superhot version of the same recipe, the Beer-Bacon Chipotle Scorpion, which throws some fiery scorpion peppers into the mix.

SECRET AARDVARK

HEAT LEVEL: 🔥🔥🔥	PRODUCER: Secret Aardvark
PEPPERS USED: Habanero	
CREATED: 2004	ORIGIN: Portland, OR

Secret Aardvark founder Scott Moritz is confidently described as a "creative and culinary genius" by the company's website. However hyperbolic the claim may be, Scott's creativity in the kitchen is clear to anyone who's tried a bottle of his Secret Aardvark Sauce. First debuted at Portland, Oregon, farmers markets in 2004, the brand has achieved a cult status among in-the-know chiliheads online. One top-performing post on Reddit's *r/spicy* forum is simply a photo of some Aardvark bottles, with the title "New favorite sauce." Each bottle features the logo of a blue aardvark in a bandit mask, snout-deep in a plastic condiment bottle (perhaps a diet of angry fire ants has prepared it for what's inside). The name comes from an in-joke that Moritz had with his childhood pals, when they convinced a local paper they were part of a fictional gang called the Secret Aardvarks. The paper then published a warning about the Aardvarks to its readers. The infamy of the Aardvark name has only grown since then.

While the company first came out the gate with ten sauces, it later scaled back to three of its most popular offerings. Newly added to the selection is the Serrabanero Green, made with a combination of serrano and habanero peppers. The blend means it's spicier than your average green sauce, and as with many artisanal sauces, its ingredients list is a bit on the long side. That's because the basic hot sauce formula is rounded out with wholesome surprises like tomatillos, apple cider vinegar, mustard seed, lime juice, and turmeric. What results is a medium-spicy, tangy sauce, with a diverse flavor profile to boot. Genius? Maybe. In any case, it's hard to deny this sauce is inspired.

SUBIACO ABBEY MONK SAUCE

HEAT LEVEL: 🌶🌶🌶🌶	PRODUCER: Subiaco Abbey
PEPPERS USED: Habanero	
CREATED: 2003	ORIGIN: Subiaco, AR

Can making hot sauce be a religious experience? The Benedictine monks at Subiaco Abbey in Arkansas certainly think so. Since 2003, they've been producing their own special recipe of habanero hot sauce, using ingredients farmed right on the monastery grounds. There is a surprisingly long history of monks growing chili peppers, dating back to the sixteenth-century Spanish and Portuguese monastics who were among the first Europeans to experiment with the culinary capabilities of chilies.

Today, the Subiaco monks base their process on techniques that Father Richard Walz learned during his time in Belize. He brought a couple habanero pepper seeds back with him and planted them in the abbey garden, where they're still harvested to this day. Walz oversees the production of the now-famous Monk Sauce, which the Subiaco monks bottle and ship around the world. According to the Subiaco Abbey website, the heat of the peppers is "enhanced by the hot and dry Arkansas summers" and, presumably, by the divine light of heaven. Their recipe is a simple and homey combination of peppers, vinegar, onions, carrots, garlic, and salt. What sets the recipe apart is that it simply uses *more* peppers, whereas larger manufacturers will skimp on the good stuff to maximize profit. Visitors to the abbey can purchase the sauce for a humble price, provided they arrange the pickup in advance. And while you're there, you can also try the Subiaco monks' other specialty—a homemade peanut brittle.

TABASCO

HEAT LEVEL: 🔥🔥	PRODUCER: McIlhenny Company
PEPPERS USED: Tabasco	
CREATED: 1868	ORIGIN: Avery Island, LA

In the 1850s, Louisiana plantation owner Maunsel White put his slaves to work manufacturing a medicinal sauce called "Maunsel White's Concentrated Essence of Tabasco Peppers." It was first unveiled at a dinner honoring the former president Andrew Jackson, and soon enough, White's unpaid workforce was delivering bulk orders all across New Orleans. Thanks to White's bombastic promotional efforts, the tabasco pepper sauce became the talk of the town. But White's success was short-lived, and he died in 1863. Inspired by White's recipe, one local banker by the name of Edmund McIlhenny began making a tabasco pepper sauce of his own. He called it simply "Tabasco Sauce."

When the Civil War ended, McIlhenny's team consisted of many formerly enslaved farmworkers. On McIlhenny's Avery Island farm, they cultivated and produced a sauce similar to White's original, which they strained into old cologne bottles. This allowed the liquid to be dispensed by the drop, a principle still in place today. McIlhenny had the good marketing sense to send samples to wholesalers across the Gold Coast and New Orleans and even up to New York. Thousands of orders started to roll in, at a whopping $1.00 per bottle (a pretty penny at the time). The sauce even made its way to England, and in 1872, McIlhenny had to open a London office to handle all the orders. It was officially an international success. Some of Tabasco's earliest advertising boasted the product was "a potent aid to digestion." It started popping up in early films, such as Charlie Chaplin's *The Immigrant*.

The bottles swapped out a cork top for its iconic red cap in 1927. Today, Tabasco-brand sauce is sold in 160 countries around the world. Throughout its success, the Tabasco recipe has remained as simple as ever—red peppers, vinegar, and salt, aged Louisiana-style in oakwood whisky barrels.

TAPATÍO

HEAT LEVEL: 🔥🔥	PRODUCER: Frito-Lay
PEPPERS USED: Unknown	
CREATED: 1971	ORIGIN: Maywood, CA

Gracing the tables of burrito joints and taco bars across the United States, Tapatío is a runny medium-heat sauce that tastes of tradition. The sauce was first introduced in 1971 by one Jose-Luis Saavedra Sr. in between working two other jobs. Originally, he named the sauce "Cuervo," as an homage to his wife Dolores Cuervo, of the famous Jose Cuervo family. However, the company was served with a lawsuit from the Jose Cuervo tequila company two years later, and the name was ditched. (Cuervo now owns the competitor brand Cholula.) The current moniker comes from a regional identifier for residents of the city of Guadalajara, Mexico, where Saavedra's kids were born.

By the end of the 1980s, increased demand for the sauce and its burgeoning appeal beyond the Hispanic community led the company to introduce ever-larger containers. In addition the ubiquitous ten-ounce bottle, the sauce is now sold in everything from individual packets to a monster gallon jug. Its iconic label was rolled out in 1997, featuring a handsome gent in a halo-like sombrero and traditional Mexican cowboy's suit called the *traje de charro*. The image now appears everywhere from memes to merchandise available through the company's website. You can even buy yourself a set of Tapatío golf balls. In 2011, Tapatío partnered with Frito-Lay on a line of sauce-flavored Doritos. To make sure the chips would sell, the Saavedras first tested them on a son-in-law with an American's sensitivity to spicy foods.

TEXAS PETE

HEAT LEVEL: 🔥	PRODUCER: TW Garner Food Company
PEPPERS USED: Cayenne	
CREATED: 1929	ORIGIN: Winston-Salem, NC

This Louisiana-style sauce was born in Winston-Salem, North Carolina, which leaves one wondering where the "Texas" part comes in. Turns out, it was nothing more than a marketing decision. In 1929, a teenaged barbecue stand operator named Thad Garner chose to call his new sauce "Mexican Joe." Thad's father Sam Garner put his foot down and insisted it should have an "American" name. So the state of Texas, formerly part of Mexico, was chosen as its namesake instead. "Pete" was a nickname belonging to Sam's brother Harold (it seems this family had a history of inexplicable naming choices). To complete the picture, a lasso-wielding cowpoke was chosen as the company logo in 1953.

The sauce was first whipped up in the Garner family kitchen and peddled by Sam across the state during the Great Depression. Today, the distributing plant still stands in the same spot as the Garner family farmhouse and is run by the descendants of the Garner clan. Texas Pete has long enjoyed a spot among the top-selling sauces in the United States. With a fairly low Scoville rating of 747, the Texas Pete original formula is a mild offering, but an offshoot called Texas Pete Hotter Hot Sauce claims to be three times as hot. The company now boasts eleven flavors total, including a Garlic Hot Sauce and Mexican-style sauce called ¡Sabor!

GOTTA STASH 'EM ALL

Collecting hot sauce has long been a cherished chilihead pastime. But which collection can claim to be the largest in the world is the subject of some debate. *Guinness World Records* currently gives the record to one Chip Hearn of Rehoboth, Delaware, an industry veteran who founded one of the original hot sauce websites, Peppers.com. However, Hearn's record may have already been surpassed by Vic Clinco, an Arizona man whose home collection numbers over 8,600 sealed bottles. After Clinco's wife gave him a gift pack of hot sauces over two decades ago, Clinco developed a full-blown obsession with expanding his sauce library. Today, it's taken over just about every square inch of wall space in his living room. The two collectors share a friendly rivalry, however, with Clinco teasing the elder Hearn that he's nipping at the champion's heels.

TORCHBEARER

HEAT LEVEL: ♨♨♨♨♨	**PRODUCER:** Torchbearer Sauces
PEPPERS USED: Habanero, ghost, Trinidad scorpion	
CREATED: 2004	**ORIGIN:** Mechanicsburg, PA

This small Pennsylvania brand is best known for its line of all-natural superhot sauces, which use the world's most notoriously hot peppers. Its superhot varieties average roughly 400,000 SHU each. For comparison, that's about a hundred times as hot as your typical bottle of sriracha. And they're all extract-free, which means the credit belongs entirely to the peppers themselves.

The project was started in 2004 by three friends (Vid, Ben, and Tim) when they saw they had some extra habaneros lying around their garden. Together they made a pepper preserve, which all agreed was better than any store-bought stuff. So they decided to bottle it. They drove off on a whirlwind road trip to purchase six hundred sixty-six (666) more pounds of habaneros and spent two weeks prepping their stash for the winter. The friends passed the next couple of years slinging their sauce at festivals and award shows, and these days, Torchbearer produces over twenty different flavors of garlic, barbecue, and hot sauces.

The Zombie Apocalypse Sauce is a carrot-based sauce, which comes packed with sixteen ghost peppers in every eight-ounce bottle. According to Torchbearer, the sauce is measured at a staggering 500,000 SHU. And it's *not even* their hottest offering. That distinction belongs to the also apocalyptically named The Rapture, advertised as being the hottest natural sauce in the world. It contains a 66.6 percent concentration of pulverized Trinidad scorpion and ghost peppers, whose heat is described as having a "slow evil build." Its Scoville rating? That would be 1.2 million.

TRADER JOE'S YUZU HOT SAUCE

HEAT LEVEL: 🔥🔥	PRODUCER: Trader Joe's
PEPPERS USED: Thai (green)	
CREATED: 2017	ORIGIN: Japan

Yuzu is a type of grapefruit-like citrus fruit, commonly found in Japanese and Korean cuisine. Its peel is the key ingredient in a fruity chili paste called *yuzukoshō*, a salt-cured condiment used in hot pot dishes and soups. It is most famously associated with Japan's southernmost main island of Kyushu, where its origins are traced through generations of mountain ascetics known as *yamabushi*. There are now mass-produced versions of the sauce across the country, as well as yuzukoshō-flavored chips and rice crackers. While Trader Joe's Yuzu Hot Sauce might not live up to the discerning standards of a mountain monk, the sauce is indeed made in Japan. Since its debut on Trader Joe's shelves, it's opened new horizons for U.S. hot sauce lovers. One food writer in *Cooking Light* gushingly called it "The One Condiment from Trader Joe's You Need RIGHT NOW."

When the bottle's flip-top lid opens, the sauce releases a fierce citrusy scent that's hard to pin down (is it lemon? lime? orange?). The consistency of the sauce is on the runny side, with bits of green pulp suspended in vinegar. When tasted, the sauce delivers a mild-to-medium heat, followed by an acidic tang that lingers after the spiciness fades. One thing to note is that the bottle runs small, at just 100 milligrams of sauce each. On the bright side, this meets the TSA standard for maximum-size liquid containers. So consider taking it on your next overseas flight. Kyushu, anyone?

VALENTINA

HEAT LEVEL: 🔥🔥	PRODUCER: Salsa Tamazula
PEPPERS USED: Puya	
CREATED: 1954	ORIGIN: Guadalajara, Mexico

Valentina is a quintessentially Mexican hot sauce. The reliable, all-purpose table sauce has a sentimental pull on those who grew up seeing it at food stands and in kitchen pantries the country over. Movie theaters in Mexico will often have a Valentina dispenser at their snack bar for moviegoers to sprinkle onto their popcorn. In 2013, the city of Juárez dealt with budget cuts by using Valentina to clean off the city's 110 bronze sculptures. Cheaper than the chemical stuff, it reportedly did the trick.

Despite Valentina's deep roots in Mexican culture, the sauce has also gained a foothold in states like California, Texas, and Illinois, as well as countries like Canada, Spain, and Germany. You can rest assured that a Mexican food joint is certifiably authentic when it stocks Valentina on its tables. The sauce typically comes in a 12.5-ounce glass bottle or its mammoth 34-ounce version, with a nonremovable flip-top lid. The red shape on the label is a map depicting the Mexican state of Jalisco, where the sauce has been made since 1960. The recipe employs local puya chilies, a small, fruity pepper variety of about equal heat to the jalapeño. There's also Valentina Extra Hot, made from the more potent chile de arbol.

Hot Sauce Name

—

HALL OF FAME

DEADLY

Lethal Ingestion

—

Scorpion Venom

—

Toxic Waste

—

Ultimate Annihilation

—

Weed Killer

—

Xtinction Sauce

GASTROLOGICAL

Butt Twister

———

Flamin' Flatulence

———

Queen of Farts

———

Rectal Rocket Fuel

———

Sir Fartalot's

MEDICINAL

Dr. Assburn's

—

Dr. Chilemeister's PhD of Pain

—

Professor Phardtpounder's
Colon Cleaner

—

Possible Side Effects

—

Hemorrhoid Helper

POLITICAL

Democrats: We're Not Perfect
But They're Nuts!

———

Dick Cheney's Bird Shot

———

Feel the Bern

———

Screw Democrats

———

Screw Republicans

———

Weapons of Ass Destruction